Narcissistic Abuse Recovery

The Ultimate Beginner's To Self Healing Emotional Plan Guide Through the Recovery Stages from Emotionally Abusive Relationships with a Narcissist To Loving Yourself Again

By Abigail Murphy

For more great books, visit:

EffingoPublishing.com

Download another book for Free

We want to thank you for purchasing this book and offer you another book (just as long and valuable as this book), "Health & Fitness Mistakes You Don't Know You're Making," completely free.

Visit the link below to signup and receive it:

www.effingopublishing.com/gift

In this book, we will break down the most common health & fitness mistakes, you are probably committing right now, and will reveal how you can quickly get in the best shape of your life!

In addition to this valuable gift, you will also have an opportunity to get our new books for free, enter giveaways, and receive other useful emails from us. Again, visit the link to sign up:

www.effingopublishing.com/gift

TABLE OF CONTENTS

Introduction 7

Chapter 1: Understanding Narcissism 9

What goes behind the head of a narcissist? 10

Many faces of Narcissism 13

Do they know that they know they know? 20

Control, control, you must learn control! 23

Chapter 2: Understanding the victim 27

Are you the next target of a Narcissist? Let's see 28

People seeking the Ultimate Relationship or Soulmates: 29

Bob the Builder 31

A need for harmony is a joy to thrive 33

High IQ 37

Extreme perfectionists with their work 38

Visualization 39

He asked for iced coffee in his cold raspy voice. 40

Chapter 3: Break-up is necessary 43

Idealization 46

Devaluation stage 47

Splitting phase 50

Discarding 50

Verbal Trickery 51

Gaslighting 53

Narcissistic Projection 55

Silent treatment of a narcissist 56

Reptilian Stare 58

Chapter 4: How to gear up for the process 59

Strategic maze 59

Social Network 62

Break the bond 63

Prerequisites for the great confrontation 65

During the great confrontation 65

Visualization 67

Chapter 5: Dealing with post breakup breakdowns 76

Asking to be recompensed 77

Wanting to know what they are up to 77

Self-Doubt 78

How to Counter All that 78
Conclusion **80**
Final Words **81**
About the Co-Authors **82**

Introduction

Mirror, Mirror on the Wall

Who is the fairest of them all?

The Mirror that shows you your regular reflection can simultaneously display the narcissist a reflection that in their eyes is fairest, smartest, and the most superior of all. If the mirror disagrees to do so, the narcissist will go out to hunt all the Snow Whites in town till the mirror complies with *their* truth. If you happen to be the Snow White of this narcissist, you are in great danger. A danger that will break you. A danger that will make you. A danger that will make you reborn.

Also, before you get started, I recommend you **joining our email newsletter** to receive updates on any upcoming new book releases or promotions. You can sign-up for free, and as a bonus, you will receive a gift. Our "*Health & Fitness Mistakes You Don't Know You're Making*" book! This book has been written to demystify, expose the top do's and don'ts and to finally equip you with the information you need to get in the best shape of your life. Due to the overwhelming amount of misinformation and lies told by magazines and self-proclaimed "gurus," it's becoming harder and harder to get reliable information to get in shape. As opposed to having to go through dozens of biased, unreliable, and untrustworthy sources to get your health & fitness information. Everything you need to help you has been broken down in this book for you to easily follow and to immediately get results to achieve your desired fitness goals in the shortest amount of time.

Once again, to join our free email newsletter and to receive a free copy of this valuable book, please visit the link and signup now: **www.effingopublishing.com/gift.**

Chapter 1: Understanding Narcissism

With increasing awareness of mental illnesses, there is now a pattern noticed among the people who toss it around and diagnose others and sometimes themselves, with mental disorders for minor inconveniences. Temporary sadness is often labeled with depression or nervous breakdown. Similarly, temporary annoyance with things out of order is labeled with Obsessive Compulsive Disorder or OCD. And similarly, self-love or self-acceptance is also sometimes confused with narcissism. People are self-obsessed and sometimes vain in the 21st century, especially when the world is driven by celebrity culture. Yet as every other disorder misunderstood, self-love is not the only criteria to fit in the puzzle of what narcissism is. There are other aspects of the disorder that often goes unnoticed. This chapter is dedicated to understanding exactly that. They are in love with a grandiose and idealized image of themselves that they keep in their mind.

What goes behind the head of a narcissist?

One might ask why they would keep such fantasies of unlimited and uncontained importance or power. Why is there an undying need for special treatment and admiration for every little task they do or things they say? How can someone love an image of themselves so much so that they delude themselves into thinking that they are that person? When probed deep inside their minds, one would find hidden among that layer of perfection, insecurities that are dark and ugly enough to cower at the exposure to light. From the inside, narcissism is tainted with unstable self-esteem that many people consider to be high. People often mistake it to be high due to genuine reasons because many psychologists have actually conducted studies where they measured the narcissist's self-esteem and found them to score high in that area. But of course, judging the book by its cover might have been a good business idea, but it doesn't work well in science. After digging deep into this matter of interest, psychologists found out that people have two kinds of high self-esteem: secure and fragile. Narcissist belongs in the latter category with their high self-esteem relying on self-deception and external locus of validation. Consider a parasite that latches onto their host and sucks admiration, attention, and validation out of them as their nutrition. That picture you just made in your mind; it is exactly how it's like to deal with them. Because the stage they build to perform their act on is built on the foundations of dysfunctional behaviors and attitudes.

The volatility and impulsivity in their behavior that ultimately leads to the arrogant, self-centered thought process and behavior often result in a display of zero empathy, which subsequently develops into an unstable interpersonal relationship. The prevalence of this disorder in the communities is rare, ranging from 0 – 6.2 percent. But around 50 – 75 percent of people clinically diagnosed with NPD are males. No wonder most women are victims at the hands of these men. A mesh of demanding, patronizing, selfish, shameless, manipulative, cocky, and unsympathetic entity garbed in human flesh is always ready to hunt for a host.

They also have a tendency to turn a blind eye to their behavior, because let's face it, the grandiosity they worked so hard to build up cannot tumble down at the slightest criticism, can it? But what if it's causing them problems and people are still standing up to them for their unjust erratic behavior? They hold up a Captain America shield and deflect the avalanche of criticisms to others; mostly to those who are standing up to them in the first place. In their world, the walls they built can never be penetrated, and so the disagreements or criticisms are a pathetic attempt at personal attacks by others. Because in the end, the mirror on the wall tells them that they are perfect, they are beautiful, and far beyond the intellectual and emotional capacity of normal people. Mostly, if someone, unfortunately, falls in love with such a person, they tend to play along with their set of demands, just so they don't get to be the victim of their rage and coldness. It's easier that way. Easier, unless their poison becomes toxic.

Many faces of Narcissism

So to get a better understanding of why they are the way they are, let's delve deeper into the many faces of narcissism. Narcissism is a spectrum, so there is no one way that it will manifest itself. But the two most important distinctions of narcissism are grandiose and vulnerable narcissism, which sometimes blends as well.

Grandiose narcissism is often considered a subclinical or mild form of narcissism because it fuses positive and negative aspects of the spectrum. The positive being high self-esteem, extraversion, charm, self-efficacy, self-confidence, and assertiveness. But obviously, it is not without its negative manifestations that might come in the form of exploitation, entitlement, disagreeableness, dominance, antagonism, and aggressiveness. For them, they have to maintain that grandiose by various means; if someone happens to befriend or court them, they often become the main object to that display.

The reality is often different than what a grandiose narcissist would consider it to be since it does not always share the grandiose version of him. To counter that, from the very start, they would start training their mind to live in a fantasy world where their supremacy, in everything, be it looks, be it intelligence, or be it social acceptability, is greater than anyone else's around them. This training doesn't happen in one day if that is what you are thinking. You can't just one day begin to think that your supremacy exceeds everyone else's, and it happens the next day. Nope. These fantasies are made to strive to become a version that is greater than everyone else, and to achieve that, a narcissist would not have any hurdle to come in between. If it does so, it is met with extreme rage and defensiveness, with their charm dwindling into rubbles.

Even in this realm of grandiose narcissism, there are two dimensions that define whether or not they would be tolerable to their partner or general society. This concept is called in scientific terms Narcissistic Admiration and Rivalry Concept (NARC). If I am to break it down and take the former chunk of the name called Narcissistic Admiration, it epitomizes the assertiveness and self-improving aspects of a narcissistic individual. In this case, the narcissist would have fantasies of grandiose, an aspiration for uniqueness, and self-enhancing behaviors that will exude a positive aura of admiration for that person, ultimately boosting his narcissistic ego.

The second dimension, however, is where the trouble begins, for that is composed of narcissistic rivalry that is constantly striving for antagonism and defense. A person overpowered with narcissistic rivalry would exude a red or black, (whatever you consider dangerous) aura, for these people will strive for supremacy via a display of hostility, and negative speech, which might belittle others in most cases. The devaluation of others gives them a sense of value. Or, if I may add, their eyes light up with excitement when they see the light diminishing from someone else's eyes. The result is nasty, more often than not, resulting in fights and conflicts.

So at one point where the first dimension leads a narcissist to have their goals directed on self-stimulation, hedonism, self-direction, achievements for which they will manifest lower distrust, forgiveness, gratitude, benign envy, grandiosity and high self-esteem; the second dimension, on the other hand, will direct the narcissist to a strive of power achieved by malicious envy, low self-esteem, the nonexistent concept of forgiveness, low trust, zero empathy, loneliness, impulsivity, and low self-esteem.

Honestly, if the second dimension weren't so cruel, it would almost be an object of pity. And since it is a spectrum, the lines to these distinctions are often blurred with time.

For example, a grandiose narcissist at the first meeting would be considered popular, competent, alluring, and charming. This deception often deludes people into thinking they are of the amiable kind, and that is how people fall into the trap of getting into a close relationship with them. But once the acquaintance turns into friendship and more, that's when the veil of charm starts to fall down and out comes the narcissistic rivalry dimension of that person, revealing their exploitative tendencies that will be bedecked with the traits I mentioned above. It's mostly a deception of the evilest kind since people almost always do not see them for the person they are because they never cross that door from acquaintance to a close relationship. They don't know what happens once the veil uncovers the actual person. They haven't seen them. And those who have had good reason to be distant to them.

Now that I have broken down the grandiose narcissism, I will uncover a darker form of the disorder that is a more clinically expressed form, called vulnerable narcissism. The roots of this form extend down to pathological fragility and distress. A vulnerable narcissist has interconnected negativity both in themselves and in their relationship with others as well. If you cross path with this kind, you will first notice anxiety, depression, mistrust, borderline traits, neuroticism, and negative temperaments in general. If you are wondering how along with all these features, do they manage to love themselves, then you might come to the right conclusion after a while, which is, they do not. And that is exactly why they feed importance and affirmation from others to absorb that nutrition of validation by others. Their minds are conflicted with poor well-being, lower self-esteem, passive aggression, hostility, avoidance, defensiveness, anxiety, incompetence, vulnerability to depression, shyness, introversion, and hypersensitivity. This emptiness that they are confronted with in their minds makes them feel entitled (rather falsely) of the validation nutrition.

Now an interesting difference between the two forms exists. A vulnerable narcissist, with all its miserably vulnerability, cannot be expected to have extraversion in their trait list. It takes guts, after all. So you cannot be deceived into thinking otherwise, as is the case with grandiose narcissism that will first lure you into their trap, only to suck the life out of you. A vulnerable narcissist, on the other hand, would trap you in his lure by the constant display of neuroticism garbed in the self-proclaimed love/care. This self-proclaimed love and care of this narcissist often delude you into feeling guilty for any negative feelings you might develop for him. And do note that he will be perfect in his attempt at making you feel that way only, for they do have secret grandiosity harboring inside them. Where one form plays the guilt card, the extrovert grandiose would belittle you and play with your self-esteem. Both forms of abuse are profound in their nature.

Moving forward, there is also a stark difference in happiness levels among these two narcissists. The vulnerable narcissist is often more clinically pronounced for the very same reason that they are challenged with more comorbidities. Anxiety and depression often come side by side, along with an extreme need to feel validated and entitled. Whereas a grandiose narcissist has lower depression levels, extreme satisfaction with themselves, and of course, a heightened love. It's almost a dream for a vulnerable narcissist to jump to the other side of the spectrum.

What connects these two separate distinctions is low agreeableness. Both are intolerable at one point. It takes time to realize that. Some people detect it earlier than others. But it does become apparent somehow. People can take bullying, threats, insults, and attacks to a certain level. The saturation capacity of every person is different. The defense mechanisms are different. The bubble that they live in so large that they think that is their world since that is all they have seen. If someone is to pop that bubble, the real world might become too much for them. To pop the bubble, or not to pop the bubble, that is the question that you have to ask yourself now.

Do they know that they know they know?

A disorder with a spectrum as wide as narcissism is still without proper treatment, be it a psychotherapeutic (treating the person with therapies) or psychopharmacological (treating the person with drugs). At least, no such experiments have been conducted as of yet. With that being said, there are no proper guidelines either that the doctors can follow.

Whatever intervention that is conducted is based on symptoms instead of the disorder itself, and guess what the most challenging aspect of the treatment would be? Yes, the acknowledgment of the disorder itself. No matter how severe the disorder is, the defensiveness and grandiosity that often comes hand in hand with narcissistic personality disorder hinder the person to acknowledge that they have vulnerabilities and problems that would require a sort of treatment to help with. So, often cases are heard where the partner of the patient recommends him or her to use the services of a therapist, but despite that, the patient would not acknowledge the problem. The problem gets worse when there are other major psychiatric disorders along with narcissistic personality disorder. Let's take into example clinical depression or bipolar disorder comorbid with a narcissism personality disorder. The element of narcissism in their traits hinder them from getting treatments for those other severe comorbidities as well. As is a common pattern observed then, the dropouts in the treatment increase, and subsequently, the symptoms might slowly alleviate than the expected period.

So now we can officially say that yes, this disorder is definitely not a monolithic entity, and that creates lots of problems for psychotherapists and diagnostician, and most importantly, the victim. Sometimes, the only clue to a person's narcissism is the victim of their abuse themselves. Thus, the relationship of a narcissist is a key diagnosis for that person. For example, certain narcissistic personalities idealize a person just to bask in the reflected glory of that idealized object. If someone tends to be beautiful or popular, the narcissistic patient would often choose them as their romantic partner just so they could flaunt them to others and receive the gratification from others that they may not deserve in general, but to them they deserve. The romantic partners thus chosen, then become subjected in full effect to their personality's conundrum, as we will see in further chapters.

Control, control, you must learn control!

Guess which Jedi Knight would take the words of Yoda to heart? Narcissists, yes. So the autonomy of their romantic partner is the first aspect that would bother a narcissist, and denying that would be their major strategy for self-gratification. How? Let's see. If their romantic partner tends to think or act independently, that would be the biggest wound to their love. Talking to another guy without telling them? Going to a yoga class instead of watching them play videogames all day? BLASPHEMY! When the terms and conditions of their romantic partner for a living do not match theirs, and when having harmless fun would mean that the partner would hurt the narcissist's honor and love, and put their conscious on a guillotine, know that the romantic partner is in trouble and that it's time to run. The hurt that they receive when the romantic partner tends to climb across the walls that the narcissist has put around their partners in the name of love and protection is immense. Control over their partners is one thing that they immensely enjoy, and the constant looming threat of their partner getting out of that control is something that always puts a narcissist on edge. So no, one may not do something as innocuous as breathe in front of a narcissist if they do not wish so, let alone fly independently. Because guess what? The control is what keeps their grandiosity alive. The control is what gives them an illusion of power that they so desperately enjoy. The control is everything for the narcissist to be able to keep their self-image intact. And in doing so, they normally forget or are unable to mentalize how much pain they are inflicting on their partner. This is where the lack of empathy comes in; they are unable to monitor the emotions of others since the only person they can satisfy is themselves. The engrossment of self makes them oblivious to the need of others, and thus they simply cannot empathize with the internal experience of others, and their need for freedom, autonomy, and agency is alien to a narcissist.

As a result of all this fiasco, what usually happens is that they start denying the responsibility of the conflicts and pain they cause to their partners and people around them. This, in turn, makes them stray away from reality, making them live in a delusional world where they cannot and are not responsible for anything.

Again, it comes in different forms. We remind again and again that narcissism is not linear but has many forms, exhibiting in many different faces. Some narcissists would have a different thought process and would attempt to manage their vulnerability in a manner that denies any sort of dependency on others. This is widely known as pseudo-self-sufficiency, which is another strategy in their catalog of grandiose maintenance. What their thought process details out to them is that they are sufficient for themselves and that they do not need others to satisfy them. Also, by doing so, they will maintain their guard. If no one can come, no one can get out, and they wouldn't have to get hurt by the added pain of losing someone. So one of the several mechanisms of coping with their grandiosity is self-sufficiency and, might I add, being proud of that. This is one way, which, more often than not, is not harmful to others. But the other type of narcissistic individuals has a way that is very often a source of exacerbation to the mental health of others. And that type is the one who refers to their love interest as a 'you complete me' object. This type of narcissist would consider themselves as incomplete and would require others (their love interest mostly) to complete them, like a hole of self-being filled with something. They would require the other person to perform the function that they themselves would miss. For example, if a person is not feeling up to the mark, they would want or rather demand their partners to soothe them, serenade them, tell they are wonderful, and show empathy for their pain. And mostly, the romantic partner is willing to do everything that they require. But the problem occurs once the partner refuses to do that, or is not consistently giving them the gratification that they feel entitled to. This halt in the praise and admiration would thus elicit the display of harmful behaviors and abuse.

CHAPTER 2: UNDERSTANDING THE VICTIM

There isn't any personality type that cannot fall prey to a toxic person, be it a narcissist, or be it a sociopath/psychopath. These people are drained of the emotion called empathy, that too, along with entitlement that exceeds all boundaries, sprinkled with a false tendency of being exploitative interpersonally to fill their cup of gains and with a sense of superiority that is most often than not, false. So be it an introvert or an extrovert, be it INFJ or anyone else with their various personality types have probably encountered once or twice, at least one such narcissist in their lifetime.

That being said, some type of personalities are often more prone to fall under the spell of a narcissist than other types of personalities. For instance, if someone possesses an INFJ personality type, then they are most likely to fall victim of psychopaths, sociopaths, and narcissists. Now, why is that? If we try to ponder over this fact, INFJ does not roam around with stickers on their forehead saying 'narcissist magnet,' do they? It is almost preposterous that someone as authentic as INFJ would get attracted to someone as inauthentic and someone as superficially pleasant as a narcissist. But then again, there are multiple reasons cataloged by researchers why these two kinds of people would initially get attracted to each other. And in this chapter we are going to explore that areas in detail, shedding light on how the interaction of the two opposite traits occurs and manifests itself, and how similar to any other type of personality, a person can be both empowered by what they have experienced throughout their interactions with the narcissist or grow more vulnerable after what they have experienced.

Are you the next target of a Narcissist? Let's see

There are multiple reasons why a narcissist might prey over a person with a certain set of traits that might come in the package of people mostly having INFJ personalities and sometimes outside of that too. Here are the reasons why.

People seeking the *Ultimate Relationship* or *Soulmates*:

Most people with an INFJ personality set are idealists. Once you are in the circle of their trust and knowledge, they would put high value onto you and put you on a pedestal that they themselves would never step on. When they are in that mental space, they will seek a type of relationship that would put their heart in the right place. What they would seek is the only thing that is ingrained in them, and they subconsciously and deep down in their mind know what they deserve – a person who would honor and respect them and choose them as they are.

When we are talking about the narcissist, there occurs an excessive bombing of love that they will display initially, which is a period when a narcissist would massively idealize and groom a subject or victim. And what does this mean for the victim? The perfect relationship they have always been asking and looking for. Their life now has all the beauty that romantic novels and movies had to give. It is perfect. It is the ultimate honeymoon phase high one needs out of a perfect relationship. All they ever asked for, be it attention, adoration, and affection; they are getting everything here from that person that they would never in their life think of getting elsewhere. It is a utopia come true for them, and they are living it every day (however few that maybe).

Since initially, the narcissist would want their subject to be charmed; they would shower words of love that might be the reason the victim would get more bewitched by the flattery presented by the narcissist. Imagine someone seeking true love and a narcissist ticking all their boxes comes along and falls into their lap (metaphorically), the false mask that they wear of guiltless admiration and innocent vulnerability, making it irresistible for the victim to not go and get that love from its roots, it is something that one can expect in this type of circumstance.

However, it's not that they are entirely deficit of judging the patterns and not learning the tools and tricks of these charlatans that they provide the victims with. It takes time for them, but once they have mastered this skill of judging these types of people, they can filter anyone giving authentic interest from their unauthentic interests.

Bob the Builder

Many times ago, I saw a picture on Twitter that described girls who had this inner tendency to need to "fix" others as "Bob, the Builders," and I would be lying if I say I didn't have a good laugh at it. There is a superpower of these kinds of victims, which sometimes (or most of the time) can become costly in terms of their mental health. And that trait is their compassion. Now compassion is used in correct amounts, and given to the right people can thrive to blossom into something beautiful. That is why earlier, I called it a superpower and not a weakness, but when narcissists are considered who have a tendency to manipulate this superpower into a weakness can be detrimental to the mental health of a victim. These sensitive kinds of people possess an enormous amount of compassionate power, and if misused, can have risks running beyond their control. These people would inherently want to help people and would go beyond their capacity to do so, just to give peace and comfort to the person that is standing next to them. Now with a normal person who appreciates what is being given to them, this behavior would make them grow themselves, and they would be thankful to the person responsible for it, but when this 'Bob the Builder' tendency is shown to a narcissist, they would not take accountability for their growth and would never acknowledge the direction of catalyst that's making them grow. In a few simple words, Bob the Builder does one thing he knows how to do, he builds; while the narcissist does one thing that they know what to do, absorb be built superficially to hide their insecurities. This superficial growth is what hinders them from being a better person in the first place, and it is in no way, the mistake of the victim. If someone is an INFJ who has been emotionally and mentally abused by this kind of narcissistic partner, they are supposed to know that it is by no fault of theirs that they are where they are.

The empathy and sensitivity might have been exploited by the narcissist partner, but the compassion that they hold is still one of the most beautiful gifts they can offer to the people of this world. What Bob the builder does is build, and it is on him/her (we are considering Bob in all sorts of genders) to either build in a more discerning manner, giving their compassion and love to people who deserve and to those who wouldn't use it to fill their own cup of gratification and entitlement.

There are people out there who are genuine enough to not take advantage of the empathy that is given to them and are grateful enough for the support they give. The key for these people is not to give a break to the boundaries built by them to meet the grand expectations of a certain narcissist who deserves not even a bit of it.

A need for harmony is a joy to thrive

Let me tell you the three Cs that a victim avoids at all costs: Conflict, Confrontation, and Chaos. Name any of these in front of them and watch blood rush to their skin and warming their cheeks, only for them to make a quick run to escape. Yes, skirting all the three Cs whenever and wherever possible is something that they most often do. And that tendency increases when they are around a narcissist since, with them, they are walking on eggshells all the time. All the survivors of abuse are prone to this behavior because of the aftereffects of trauma. Still, the victims are even more prone to minimizing, denying, and rationalizing the conduct of abusers so that they can upkeep their superficial definition of 'peace' in their mind. They would agree to the unrealistic demands and questions of the abusers just to not make themselves see the side of the narcissists they would not want to see. They would do everything and anything in their immediate control to calm the situation down so as not to let it escalate into something that they would not be able to control.

I would like to introduce here, a small concept of 'gaslighting' that the narcissists often use, which makes the victim think that any mistreatment or wrongful behavior that they believe they received at any time in the past has been in their head throughout this time and that the sensitivity and intuition that keeps on warning them about the imminent danger lying in front of them that might be a display of unhealthy behavior are in reality futile and all a creation of their fantasy. The abusive people that surround the victim may lead him or her to believe that they are either being too sensitive or too irrational. The former claim can be a little true since these victims are, in fact, sensitive, but the latter claim is entirely untrue since victims are anything but irrational. Their critical thinking power and their recognition power when the set boundaries are crossed are keen enough to not let any kind of doubt flying around their head.

And with that being said, once the victim gathers enough courage to gather their evidence, explore the nooks and corners of the problematic behavior displayed and pile them up in their mind neatly, actually mouthing out those thoughts would take a huge amount of courage, and they may very often, continually apologize for the words they are saying, scared out of their mind if they elicit chaos in return.

The problem that the victim encounters is that once they start apologizing to their narcissist partner continually, even though they had held not short discussions but ones that took a very long time to wind up makes them start ignoring the voice that keeps telling them that the relationship they are in is in reality not okay, to begin with. They are not too sensitive; the person in front is insensitive and sensitive only when the control they have is not going to be exerted on the subject anymore. Control is all they have over the person whom they call their partner, but once that control starts to shake up, and when the victim begins to find a voice of their own, they make sure that they take that voice out and quieten everything that tells the victim otherwise.

The emotional drainage that they feel is, in fact, a product of the narcissist fulfilling his basic need to rid himself of the underlying emptiness that he feels. And this act is achieved frequently by them with a few tricks up their sleeve. They frequently choose a victim who is, in fact, very easily charmed, trapped, and seduced. Too bad that an INFJ fits in all of these criteria.

High IQ

This is not necessarily in concordance with the personality of an INFJ, but another trait that is often correlated with being a narcissist's victim is being highly intelligent. Although one can express their wonder since highly smart people can look through inside a person. But most often than not, high IQ comes with low EQ, and low EQ is all they are looking for. Narcissist seeks a person who might be passionate, enthusiastic, and bright in their academic arena, but once they fall into the emotional realm, the narcissist would overpower them. The challenge is what feeds them as well. So although a high IQ is not the criteria to fit into the narcissist prey list, these people, if they encounter one as a partner, are prone to fall into the narcissist's spell.

Extreme perfectionists with their work

Once again, the perfectionists often come up with the belief that their work, no matter how good it is, will never reach the potential and the scale where it can be called perfect. And their definition of perfect is hazy, but in reality, it means 'better' than what they have done at any moment. This means that they are always going to put more effort yet will never believe in their work that they execute, which is again a perfect combination for a narcissist. Since he can manipulate the victim into believing that the efforts she has been putting in the relationship haven't been good enough and that she can always do better and better, not knowing when the level of perfection that she thought she could achieve would lie, he can use that to his advantage. Plus, the low self-esteem and anxiety that comes along with not doing enough is an added benefit to their condition, which again works in the assistance of the narcissist to fill his empty cup.

Visualization

Let me give you a visualization scenario to gather the picture from a victim's side. Imagine a narcissist, let's call them the 'Unfeeling.' So the Unfeeling would visit the victim, grab them by the waist, pin them to the wall, spit on their face and leave, leaving the door unbolted. Now the relationship had been going on for quite a long while, and by this time, the victim is used to this behavior. What would the victim do in this case? The victim scours through the cold town that night, searching for a little warmth with "it's all over" as her mantra running around her head. But she was not complying with the instructions in the head, you see. It was not over. After all, the Unfeeling came back again, let's say at 9 am. She also used to call him a Peacock, for the combination of arrogance and beauty that he possessed. With the sight of him there back again, her heart was again alighted with flame. She asked him whether he needed a tea or coffee. She calmed the invisible audience looking at her, told them not to raise their eyebrows at her. She implored them and justified her actions by saying it was her etiquette, her love, or her foolishness. She did not know yet.

He asked for iced coffee in his cold raspy voice.

She smiled and asked him, "As cold as your heart, sir?"

He blinked twice with his inky lashes entwined. She knew he made that gesture when he disapproved of her humor. She knew him throughout, yet she was not able to describe him. For her, he painted her sky more gray than blue, had a stance of IMTOOGOODFORYOU. He was a charcoal painting of a rose, and an animated toy. His rainbows had no color. She couldn't figure out if she was in love with him or not. Whether she fell out of it and was now just a formality that she was following, or she was in trouble. She was thinking all of that while he interrupted her thoughts by saying, "I come in peace." Peace was something she could not fathom attaining at that point. Little did he know that she couldn't even afford it. In her mind, she had swords unsheathed and descended the mountains while beheading trees and mountains alike. Her heart has been wrenched too many times now that she did not know what peace even sounded like. Her presence only knew violent storms and crashing waves. She never knew the heart she had so gladly given to her master would be tossed away with such ease. The heart came back to her wounded and scarred. She wanted to call it a martyr or a soldier's pride but hesitated to say so. She kept it and comforted it, promising herself that she would not let it go back to him as a refugee. She voiced out all her thoughts—every word in a clear voice.

He smiled in return, the smile that formed a depression on his cheeks. She had a love-hate relationship with that dimple, but she tried not to focus on that. He cleared his throat. "If that is your wish, be that as it may. I just came here to see you and check up on you. But I would give a little tip to ease your ablaze mind here. Do not throw away your heart to people who you do not know. Its rightful place is after all with you." And with that, he left, making the victim second guess her thoughts again and again. Did she not know her partner at all? Maybe if she gets to know him, she can undo the damage her relationship has suffered. Maybe she is not trying hard enough. Maybe once she clears her mind and puts more effort, she can again gain his positive side. Maybe he was never negative at all. And thus continues the avalanche of self-doubt. The doubts are what the narcissist is very efficient in establishing in their partner. Once the seed of doubt has been ingrained in the mind of the victim, he needs to just tick it off once in a while and see the magic of the victim coming back again and again. The ruthlessly critical behavior that is often topped with them being dismissive can work wonders on the empathetic and sensitive mind of the victim. Another key strategy of the narcissist is to switch their behavior ranging from loving and charming to being callous and indifferent. It baffles the victims, making them doubt their own judgment of the other person, thinking they are the source of transition in that person.

CHAPTER 3: BREAK-UP IS NECESSARY

There is a person who needs love more than the partner you think you are/were in love with. And that person is YOU.

There are many things that a narcissist can make you feel. It can be disoriented, deceived, debilitated, devalued, detached, discarded, distressed, disillusioned, depressed, dissociated, and dehumanized, which might sometimes even lead to suicidal ideation. But what even happens in the middle? How can things go so wrong that one ends up in such a circumstance?

There are many emotions to process throughout the relationship, and it is anything but easy. At times you want to be with him and love him. But there are times when you want the abuse to stop. Then come the times when you believe that it is all your fault. However, the feeling that remains predominant is the one that tells you that you should leave him.

He attempts to project his faults on to you so that you feel guilty for things that he did in the first place. A confusion ensues in mind, for he was nice at first and suddenly turned cruel. Questions start to pop up in mind. Is he rude? Is he trying to harm you? Or was he innocent as he said he was, and it was just you thinking it was intentional?

If these questions are popping up, then mind you, they are genuine. The actions are not accidental but premeditated, but yes, he is innocent in his own eyes.

The victim loves the narcissist since that is the kind of man he presented himself to be in the beginning, but slowly and gradually and without the acknowledgment of his tendencies, the narcissist makes the victim his source of filling the narcissistic supply cup of validation and gratification.

For a victim, this relationship is like injecting themselves with poison and dying a slow death. The misery that the narcissist feels is projected onto the victim, for he could not fathom anything otherwise. Being with a narcissist tends to be scary since a narcissist lives in a bubble of make-believe reality, which for him is ego-puffing. It is constructed by him to survive in this life without having to face his self, his cup that is empty. When such a person is with you, he would always want to show himself superior to the victim, no matter what the task or argument is about.

There are three stages to the relationship dynamics with a narcissist, which are interchangeable and mostly repetitive.

Idealization

Devaluation

Discarding

Once the victim goes through these stages, a condition is triggered known as 'Narcissistic Victim Syndrome,' which unlike domestic abuse is not visible with physical marks. Still, the mental marks that are imprinted on the mind of the victim are displayed in a wide spectrum, which sometimes cumulates to suicide as well.

Idealization

This stage is a focused and intense chase. Narcissists are mostly hyper-focused and demonstrate concern and compassion for an individual's feeling in these moments. The victim is often developed gradually to be the source of supply of gratification and validation. One may refer to it as the love-bombing phase, which evokes the delusional feeling of a soulmate in the victim. This illusion and effect are often executed to trap the person into the relationship.

Thus, the first stage in which the narcissist is in his oh-so-charming phase is called idealization. In this phase, a person attributes exceedingly positive qualities to another person. This is the moment where a narcissist would get to know the victim to attain their trust and love and condition them to remove their walls with them.

This can manifest in many ways, be it romantic trips with them, or showering beautiful words and flowers and doing these little things that would make the other person hopelessly fall in love with them.

Devaluation stage

This stage is the start of an eye-opening reality where the relationship you thought was beautiful starts to show its ugly side. The narcissist starts to appear condescending, and the relationship that was initially sacred is now disregarded. The negative and cruel side surfaces and then begins the mental abuse episodes which are manifested in the form of gaslighting, silent treatment, projection, reptilian stare, and smear campaigning in which blackmailing would ensue to display himself in the eyes of others as the victim, instead of the other way round.

The flipping of coin would make the victim see emotions that they could not fathom would come from someone that they initially idealized. The hate, anger, and disdain being exhumed from someone the victim loved come in the form of narcissistic rage as soon as the initial mask is taken out. The bond, closeness, accountability, and responsibility, everything goes down the drain, and the victim does not even get time to process it all. The idea of accountability is alien to him, and the idea of a relationship was for the victim to serve him and not the other way round or even at equal. The expectation that is withheld from such a relationship is often responded with rage, gaslighting, and avoiding. The true colors become apparent now more than ever. The fragmented illusions that were imprinted in your mind started to get disillusioned, and slowly and gradually, the victim starts to see the person for the narcissist they are. After the gradual hate for the other person, comes the self-hate in a victim for allowing the person to get inside their head like that, feeling ultimately powerless and hopeless to change the situation they are in since they are completely in love with them. The victim becomes useless for a narcissist once they start questioning the validation and gratification supply, and once they do that, the narcissist starts attributing negative qualities to the victim. If we delve deep into the brain of a narcissist, the stimulation of reward system no longer occurs, and with that not happening in terms of their partner, they turn emotionally spaced out and would not be able to move forward in the relationship towards the stage where the two could bond. Since the dopamine upsurge has diminished to the point of no return, and no positive feelings are coming out of the relationship, the narcissist starts to disconnect himself from the relationship. The mask of the perfect right man has now been taken off, leaving the victim confused more than ever.

Splitting phase

There comes a mid-phase as well, which is known as splitting. This stage is described as a phase where your mental space is bifurcated into two, dividing it into a good and bad phase. On one side is sunshine and flowers, days are filled with positivity, and idealization is at its peak. The victim feels like a queen in her very average ordinary circumstances. On the other hand, there occurs devaluation and a display of contempt. Thus the victim splits their emotions, feeling rather confused.

Discarding

So let me bare the truth right out for the victims. When the narcissist started this relationship, it wasn't to have a partner giving equal love and respect, it was for a partner filling his supply of validation and serving him with his demands of compliments, admiration, and praise whenever he needed it, which most often than not is all the time, or else the fragile bubble that they so carefully constructed would burst out, and the purpose of the relationship for the narcissist would be over.

The victim often fails to understand the relationship was never about them or their interests. The emptiness of feelings for the other person doesn't allow him to care for any other person that's not him. The things that are important to the victim don't matter since the narcissist never bothered to care for any of those. Their first agenda in the mind after you do not fulfill his cup is to discard and get rid of the victim, and for that, a multitude of techniques would be applied by him to get the victim into a mental haze.

Verbal Trickery

The narcissist knows the victim is now in their lure and that too useless for him, which gives him now a purpose to keep her in a condition of mental haze, and in a state where he persuades her to feel foolish. The goal of a narcissist is to make the victim doubt her reality and her truths that she held on to for a while. He would make all the attempts to get her to live in numerous realities, in which the narcissist reigns in almost all of them. There is a difference in characters that a victim observes; at times, she would feel like she is talking to Dr. Jekyll, while at other times, she would feel like she is talking to Mr. Hyde.

At a lot of times, she would hear words like, "I was just joking, you're taking it way too seriously," "It's all in your head," or "Well, I am like that, you have to deal with it." These phrases come too easily from someone who doesn't understand its effect on the other person. This technique is called Verbal Trickery that a narcissist often uses to exploit the victim relentlessly in a desperate attempt to baffle and gaslight the victim, making them feel guilty for actions that were not in their control.

There is a term widely used in clinical settings called 'salad' which refers to the speech pattern that is rather disordered and indicates certain illnesses like autism spectrum, dementia, bipolar disorder, and schizophrenia. A narcissist uses a similar word salad and deciphering that is concordant with searching a way out of a maze. One of the identifying factors is lack of logic, repetition, circular conversations, extensive generalizations, unrelated and disjointed use of words that go beyond the context of conversations, and suggest contradictions. One can observe deficiency of semantic fluidity, and that is what is essential for him in confusing the victim enough to never allow her to get out of that mental cage he has put her in.

Gaslighting

Here comes one of the most common forms of abuse used by narcissists termed as 'gaslighting.' It is the strongest type of emotional abuse used by a narcissist to ingrain in the victim the extremist sense of stress and anxiety, making them confused. This behavior goes on to the point; the victim can no longer trust their discerning mental capacity. It is often termed as the most covert form of exercising control over someone, making a victim feel brain-scattered and crazy.

Knowingly or unknowingly, the narcissist knows how to kill a person's confidence. Although at first, the glow in the victim would intrigue them, soon, he also figures out that that glow should never be enough to outshine the narcissist. So if it is not lower than him, then he would work meticulously to make it so, and in the process, he would make the victim doubt her own emotional and mental competence. After draining your cup of positive emotions, the narcissist would fill it up with insecurity, sadness, and self-doubt. Twisting the facts and questioning the evidence are skills that a narcissist has mastered for a very long time. And that way, the victim becomes the oppressor and oppressor, the victim, the most wonderful exchange of roles ever played out in history. At first, if there is something that might make him feel guilty, it would be immediately hidden by him. But if there is something that cannot be hidden, then he would do what he usually does all the time to himself; he would lie, skillfully and faithfully, in a manner that is confident enough to make the other person think twice about his or her reality. The purpose of this gaslighting technique is to target the self-esteem, self-confidence, and mental health of a person, rendering them unable to function stably in a healthy manner.

What the narcissist usually do is systematically withhold facts and accurate information while replacing it and feeding the victim with other inaccurate information. This replacement would then discredit the truths and facts of the victim, making them appear crazy and insane in their own eyes. The victim starts to undermine their mental capacities and believe the version of the truth the narcissist presents to them subconsciously. The abuse that is happening to them does not seem like abuse, and that is the majorly the reason why these victims would not seek help in the first place because the narcissist makes them believe that they don't need it and that they are bringing them upon themselves.

Narcissistic Projection

This technique is another means of emotional manipulation used by the narcissist, which is difficult to identify, spot, and explain. It is used as a coping mechanism to deflect responsibility of their actions, traits, and behavior by attaching it to someone else. This would give the narcissist a way to stray and avoid accountability and ownership. There is one core belief of a narcissist around which his reality is based; narcissists can never be wrong while the other person can always be wrong. He makes the victim believe that his faults are that of the victim and the guilt that he should feel is projected on to the innocent victim. The projection that is emitted on to the victim is not just of the faults and failings of acts and conducts, but it is a projection of emotions, feelings, and beliefs onto and into the victim. They project it into their heads, into their soul, and into their existence. They make sure the victim internalizes every fault of the narcissist, till their emotions are too uncontrollable to strategize.

The toxic guilt that he has about himself is projected into you since, in his world, he cannot do or be anything else but good, and if anything of lower quality is to enter his life, then it's their fault.

Silent treatment of a narcissist

Although at this point, we know that even narcissist has their pains that they cannot process. And when there's something that they cannot process, they make sure they never deal with it and avoid it at all costs. The narcissists in their childhood have never invested the same amount of time and effort to mourn over the trauma they received in their childhood. They never experienced and felt absolute sadness because they masked it with a different reality and topped it with unprocessed rage and anger. And this rage and anger sometimes spring up as the famous silent treatment of theirs.

This silent treatment is a childish manner to deal with the situations that they would rather want to avoid, which usually comes up with a lie that they could not project or a fault they could not avert. The silent treatment is a means of expressing rage towards the victim, something that is deeply-rooted and ingrained from childhood trauma, going unprocessed for decades and is now surfacing up in the relationship. It is displayed to the victim as the product of mistake caused by them.

Sometimes when he is not able to verbally shut up the victim, it is then when he uses this technique to punish and manipulate the person into agreeing with them, trying to suffice it with his lack of communication skills, giving the victim a form of abuse that is silent. This kind of technique is used by those who haven't matured emotionally.

Reptilian Stare

Sometimes when a victim looks into the eyes of his abuser, what she sees, staring back at her instead, is two icy black holes staring back at her, fully devoid of emotion. This nothingness and lack of emotion in the eyes is an indicator of their empty cup of feelings. Although this icy stare is used to intimidate a person into succumbing to their commands, yet a person could measure the lack of soul just by gazing at the eyes. The reason for mentioning this specific kind of stare is that many victims do not notice how the oppressor affects to the extent that they can control the arguments if not verbally then through eyes only. If one just starts to notice that, they can assess the rest of the personality very easily.

CHAPTER 4: HOW TO GEAR UP FOR THE PROCESS

To be brutally honest with all the victims out there, even acknowledging the fact that they need to break up is the hardest thing to swallow in their entire life, and I know it. Narcissists are a kind of vampire that sucks energy instead of blood out of a person. They can make a person fall in love with them so deeply that it mostly feels like if a victim leaves them, they will leave behind a part of themselves.

But there are certain measures to be taken if one needs to climb back from the hole that they have fallen in so recklessly.

Strategic maze

If the narcissist gets a whiff of someone taking enough control of their life to untie the knots of relationship with them, they will make every attempt in their conscious control to make the other person stay. Now, remember, resisting these attempts are not going to be easy, especially after all that the victim has been through, they will have to be strategic.

Breaking up with a narcissist is a person inflicting "narcissistic injury" to them, which most of the times induce a narcissistic rage. Thus keeping all the safety measures in mind, it is essential to create a physical and emotional escape plan beforehand to ensure that the victim gets an ample amount of skills to cope up in the aftermath. If the victim finds their usual abusive partner suddenly getting affectionate and warm towards them, it is possible that they sensed you withdrawing yourself emotionally to become powerful. The best way out of this is not to give them a hint about the predictable departure; the victim can act in a manner that shows them to be preoccupied with other tasks and projects or just busy in something that might not make them suspicious.

A method is known as "Grey Rock Method" is a method where the victim can act emotionally unreactive in times when the narcissist attempts to provoke them;

using this method would make the narcissist slow down and lay back momentarily.

During this time, if the victim is cohabiting or is married to their oppressor, they can get an ample amount of time to seek the support of lawyers, gather finances, and build resources to cope up with the sense of independence. The coping resources could range from searching for local communities like yoga or meditation centers, and finding local shelters serving domestic violence victims. The reason that you are in a relationship with a narcissist does not, in any way, mean that you cannot kick-start healing and look for connections that are beyond the relationship you already have. On the other hand, doing so would make their resolve for breakup stronger since they will then encounter people who would be genuinely loving and respectful and would open their eyes to the world outside of oppression and hate.

Social Network

The first thing that a victim is drained during their relationship is energy. The energy to interact with people, the energy to work, and the energy to build other relationships. The isolation that a narcissist puts his victim in has a tendency to make the victim feel like that that is the only reality in their lives at that point. They need to pop that bubble and let themselves escape and step out of it to make a support network, which would help them cope up with the problems in their relationship. Even if one does not find good people out there, there are still online forums ranging from personalized coaching on Skype to Facebook groups for victims of emotional and mental abuse where one can get the support they need to uplift themselves psychologically to get out of the situation they are in. There are meetups held, formed based on types of abuse the group of people faces. There are many resources out there to be able to get help from, some more fine-tuned and well-vetted than others, but they exist and are inclusive of all kinds of people. Some people might not have experienced exactly what the victim is experiencing, but they can still relate and bond to the pain they are feeling. And that bond is what helps them form healthy relationships with those people, and empathy starts to flow in from every direction till they are forced to see the brighter side to their dark world. Hence, joining such groups and reading thoroughly the articles of narcissistic abuse that they post, watching experts and advocates talk about it, and engaging with other survivors to know what they did in their situation is of immense importance if one needs to get out of the abuse bubble and engage in self-care. Once the victim gets enough acknowledgment and validation, then this violence they receive would eventually be stopped. The first and foremost measure to be taken is to make the victim realize that they are not alone in this and that people are out there waiting for them to escape so that they may hold their hands and walk with them to a better world.

Break the bond

There forms a bond based on trauma shared between the victim and its abuser, one that is built on strong emotional experiences. That bond is strong enough that even making a slight mark on it can make the victims scared out of their minds. Then how must a victim proceed with this gesture? Trust me; they wouldn't need to make much effort into this for their reality would be enough of a reason to make them realize the intensity of toxicity that has developed in their partner. They just need to acknowledge these facts, which could be done by writing the abusive occurrences down to ensure there isn't any abusive amnesia working in the victim's mind when the narcissist in their loving phase. Certain counselors are well-versed in traumatic incidents; talking to them can make the relationship dynamics with the abuser clearer, making the victim identify the tactics that an abuser uses. However, finding the right therapist is immensely important, for not everyone is skilled in dealing with a survivor of abuse. And if a therapist invalidates them, then there's a chance, the victim might step down a darker hole of depression. Engaging with a coach and a trauma counselor who understands the dynamics of narcissistic abuse are the only ones to be sought here.

Prerequisites for the great confrontation

There is something at the biggest stake for the narcissist when the victim would have the inevitable conversation of breaking up, and that is "PRIDE." It wouldn't matter what the victim has planned up and how cautious they are; once the narcissist feels rejected, he will automatically feel a humiliation they would try to counter. In the attempt to counter the humiliation, he will assert dominance in the conversation, which will again trigger all the fear reflexes that they have ingrained in the victim, making her doubt her conviction. In times like these, the victim needs to limit the time she will spend with the partner or make a trusted person stand near her while she moves forward with the confrontation so that she doesn't feel threatened or alone.

During the great confrontation

Although you may have heard the quote 'honesty is the best policy,' but that would be the most foolish idea to work with when dealing with a narcissist. Yes, it may sound deceptive and cowardly, but being direct while confronting a narcissist will always go wrong. The conversation needs to be framed in a way that describes narcissist's benefit out of it, rather than the victim's. Thus a sentence like, "I can't do this anymore' is foolish to say, but "I believe this relationship isn't giving you as much happiness as you thought it would," or that "It's not working out for either of us," is not foolish. Blame is an important element here that one needs to avoid at all costs no matter how strongly the victim feels about it since the world of narcissist does not know any faults in himself, and the victim is showing them that would become an enemy really quick. Their defense tactics would again start working up, and we all know how smart narcissists get when they play their defense game. So no matter how intensely you need to prove a point to him, do not. He is not worth it.

***

The breakup is hard. It is like surgery for heartbreak, and you are the patient being treated.

Visualization

~ "Hello victim, you will be undergoing two separate surgeries today. One heart surgery and one brain surgery." She told herself while looking in the mirror. The kitchen knife in her hand didn't look like a normal surgical scalpel, but she knew she had no other options. She couldn't afford to bare her soul for such extensive procedures. She knew that no doctor would be more competent than her for what she was about to do.

"Okay, Miss Casey, the first procedure, will be your heart surgery. I know I am not the best surgeon in the hospital, but I assure you, no one can understand the procedure YOU need as I do. I know where the injuries are, and I know what will fix those injuries because I was half responsible for every one of them. You have no choice but to trust me. So how about you make this procedure pleasant and don't sabotage our patient-doctor relationship by being doubtful and skeptical? I know your heart is precious to you, but I'll make sure you don't die during the process. Also, we will be using the minimum amount of anesthesia for this process. You have to understand the pain; you have to go through it completely to understand and to appreciate the peace that will come out of this if you survive it completely. The hold he has on you will be gone." She told the patient casually; the fear was etched in the creases of the patient's forehead and the wrinkles around her eyes. The fear of the unknown, the fear of letting go of the life that she knew so well and was used to, the fear of there being no anchor of pain to hold her down in her past. Yet, the patient knew her heart was dying slowly. She needed the surgery. She had to trust the doctor.

"Okay, but can you at least make my body paralyzed so that I don't harm myself if the pain becomes too much?" The victim asked in a small voice.

"Of course, I will be injecting Atracurium from time to time because I don't need your resistance at any point." The doctor was least bothered. She had never been this hard on any patient, but this was a patient she never showed leniency towards. She treated her so brutally that all her humanity went out the door.

"Let's take you to the operation table, and as you will be fully awake, I will be explaining all the steps to you."

"Please be gentle." Her plea would go unnoticed, the victim knew, but she still had to voice her concern.

"Let's strip away your skin with your clothes, my dear victim. This stupid piece of skin is too thin; everything gets under it easily. Let's change it as well. From now on, your skin will be tough as leather. I have ordered a new one. It will be arriving shortly." The doctor injected the muscle relaxant and started marking her skin with a black marker. As she was lying down on the kitchen table, the victim thought the marking process would last for hours, but suddenly she felt the knife cutting through her skin. She wanted to scream but she couldn't. Her throat felt paralyzed. And before she knew it, the skin of her right arm was completely gone. The muscles and ligaments could all be seen along with the blood. She wanted to faint, but the pain was too unbearable to allow unconsciousness. It didn't take the doctor long, and in a matter of half an hour, her skin was gone. She was not dead, which surprised her. Apparently, the doctor knew what she was doing because her promise to not kill her was still intact. Her eyes could only sense the redness of the muscle and blood. Red was the only color in her mind now. She knew she would never get rid of red again.

The doctor used a small bone cutter to open her rib cage. She knew she wouldn't survive the operation. But suddenly, the doctor injected something in her arm, and her pain was not as much as it was before. "Bitch," her mind was calling the doctor bitch the entire time. She couldn't remember any other cuss words for the life of her! It was useless to think about those, though, she couldn't speak.

The cracking of the bones was too loud now, and her ribcage was now open on the left side. The doctor had never seen an open ribcage surgery in real life, so she had only YouTube videos to rely on. But she knew the victim would never sue her. She would even be thankful one day for this sanity-saving procedure. The site of the beating heart brought on a flood of memories for both the victim and the doctor. It reminded them of the time when their heart used to beat without pain and fear. Freely and completely.

The doctor was hesitant in touching the hart; she knew one mistake could lead to death. She knew she had protected her heart like a lioness protects her cubs, but she also knew that her heart was conquered and then slashed, despite all the efforts. The doctor thought about putting the victim under full anesthesia, but there was no team of anesthetists to help her. She didn't want to take the risk. The victim would survive, she always had.

"I'll be touching your heart now, my dear victim. It will be painful, more than anything else that you have ever been through, but it will be okay by the time we are done. Trust me." The doctor tried to calm both of their nerves down.

The doctor then calmly used the tiniest blade she could find in the hardware store and proceeded to make the incision between the two ventricles of the heart. She didn't want to reach the natural pacemakers of the heart directly. She started from the apex of the heart and reached the middle of the interventricular septum and stopped. She used her fingers to open the heart gently. Thankfully her grandmother's suctioning machine was still working and was sucking the pouring blood nicely with the help of a large diameter nasogastric tube. She knew she would have to empty the jar at some point in the toilet during the operation, but she wasn't going to worry about that. She opened the heart in the safest way possible for her. She had cut and eaten a lot of cows' and chickens' hearts, and since she was the one who used to clean meat in her house, she knew how to open the heart without destroying its structure.

She then saw the slash in the inner portion of the heart and some broken chordate tendinae, strings that attached different parts of the heart. Casey was 25; there was no way her heart was broken by natural causes. It had heartbreak written all over it. The doctor wanted to punch the causative human being, but she knew it was her fault as well as his. She let him in; she let him get in control of her. But how she wished that she could have the chance to do the same surgery on the causative agent as well. She would have shown him what heartbreak and pain of oppression means. She wouldn't have even used a muscle relaxant on hi, she would have used belts to hold him in place. But meh, she was a doctor, revenge was not supposed to be a part of her thought process. But ah, it would have felt so sweet. "Focus, damn it." She said loudly, which scared the victim out of her damned existence.

"Okay, my dear victim, I see some broken heartstrings and a slash in the innermost layer of your left ventricle. This is the price you pay for keeping someone so oppressive deep inside of you. This should teach you not to be stupid enough to love without expectations. This should also show you how your idiotic decisions have led you to this point. I am going to cut all the strings out in that area and remove them permanently. It will decrease the efficiency of the functioning of your heart as these strings are attached to your papillary muscles to the posterior cusp of your mitral valve. In short, you had kept him so deep inside that he was not even visible to you on the front. Damn it, victim, you stupid fool! Anyway, you will not be able to get enough blood in your body, and your heart will always make weird sounds now. But this had to be done. I am going to repair the tear, and then I am going to place a 'no-go area' sign on your heart." The doctor's frustration could be heard from her voice.

The doctor completed the procedure and then thought about what she should do with the valve; she didn't have any prosthetic valves on her. So she decided to place a metallic sheet and replaced the broken pieces and cut off strings with very fine elastic tubes.

She knew there was a great chance the body would react very strongly against it; she knew the patient wouldn't be able to survive if the body developed sepsis. She knew the tissue rejection would be too much. But she also knew that hardening the pieces of the heart that were too soft, to begin with, would be her best bet to survive. At least, the next time, she wouldn't be attacked in the same place.

"Okay, my dear victim, I have replaced a few things with stronger material in your heart. It won't be broken from those sites now, at least. You are too stupid to not fall in love with someone like that again, but at least one part of your heart would be strong enough to survive the heartbreak. I am going to allow you to recover now after I have closed your ribcage. Your skin won't be replaced for a few days, though, you need to feel everything to the extreme extent in order to develop a strong desire for the thicker skin. Otherwise, you'll keep rejecting change, and you'll keep on falling back to the old patterns." The doctor said coldly and resumed her business, leaving the victim to dread the coming days. Deep down, the victim knew the doctor wanted what was best for her. But she also knew the doctor wouldn't show her the same humanity she would show to anyone else. Because the victim was the doctor, and the doctor was the victim. She had been heartbroken by the narcissist, and she had decided to rectify the mistake. No prisoners were allowed, only brutality and endings. The victim had to undergo a brain evacuation as well, and she didn't think she would survive that. Or maybe she would. The doctor always knows the best.

CHAPTER 5: DEALING WITH POST BREAKUP BREAKDOWNS

After getting your sense of self completely ripped off by the narcissist, you will be exposed to the hefty task for rebirthing yourself once you have left them.

This task will be time-intensive, and it will require you to stand up to your demons and send them off to hell. These demons are the memories left to you by the narcissist. These are the scars that they have left on your body. These demons also manifest themselves in the form of false and demeaning beliefs about who you are. All of these demons will need to be expelled so that you can give yourself a new and better life.

The recovery will be troubled with obstacles. You will experience feeling as if you are leaping big leaps of faith, and you will feel good about it, but then there will come a time when you would feel like nothing has changed in you. You still need them in your life, with all their toxicity. You would feel that somehow their poisonous company was better than their absence.

Asking to be recompensed

You would often feel the urge to avenge your hurt. You would want to do something one way or the other to get back at your abuser, the one who destroyed life for you. But even then, your rational side of the brain would know that this urge only means that you are not ready to let them go from your life. It knows, deep down, that you seek their participation in your life, you seek their involvement, and you seek their attention. However, recovery from this sense of dependence is what you need. Therefore, it's better to leave the past behind and let it rest behind you.

Wanting to know what they are up to

You will experience distress, and you won't sit still until you know what the abuser is doing, how he or she is doing, and which emotional state they are in. It will suddenly and unintentionally become more about them than you. You will easily fall victim to the wrath of social media. You would start stalking them; you would start hitting up their friends to know more about them. It will just become something that you have to do, and you can't breathe without getting it done. But instead, what it will do is it will create a rift in you where all the memories will come flooding back in.

When you see that they are living life to their fullest, you would feel emotional stabs, and it will upset you even more because now you are not part of their life anymore.

Self-Doubt

The next phase of emotion is that you will start doubting yourself. You would start questioning yourself and admonishing the very fact that you were unable to detect and count the red flags. You would feel stupid and manipulated. You would see things as clear as day now, but you would not forgive yourself for not seeing them before. You would forgive yourself one day and then beat yourself the next.

What could be worse is this: you won't trust yourself ever to trust any other person again. Ever. You would imagine a solitary life, and you would shun your prospects, and you would feel that living alone is much better than being disappointed all over again.

How to Counter All that

The best way to recover from narcissistic abuse is to let them stay in the past. Do not revisit their memories. If you do find yourself amidst the emotional phase where you need them, just pick a book, hit up a chat with a close friend, go to a charity event or attend an art gallery. Busy yourself with just about anything else than remembering the moments with the narcissist. It will do you wonders, not in a month, maybe not in a year, but you will get it together. And you will one day arrive at a point, where their name doesn't leave a poisonous taste in your mouth, it doesn't send your brain to the dark alleys. It just becomes a name, someone you knew, but someone who doesn't have any control over you.

CONCLUSION

You cannot fix a narcissist, do not try to. It is a personality disorder for a reason. If they are not willing to change or control their abusive tendencies, if they are not even acknowledging their mistakes and going to a psychotherapist, there's a fair chance that you would fail in that attempt too. So run. And run away, smartly.

Final Words

Thank you again for purchasing this book!

We hope this book can help you.

The next step is for you to **join our email newsletter** to receive updates on any upcoming new book releases or promotions. You can sign-up for free, and as a bonus, you will also receive our "*7 Fitness Mistakes You Don't Know You're Making*" book! This bonus book breaks down many of the most common fitness mistakes and will demystify many of the complexities and science of getting into shape. Having all this fitness knowledge and science organized into an actionable step-by-step book will help you get started in the right direction in your fitness journey! To join our free email newsletter and grab your free book, please visit the link and signup: **www.effingopublishing.com/gift**

Finally, if you enjoyed this book, then we would like to ask you for a favor, would you be kind enough to leave a review for this book? It would be greatly appreciated! Thank you, and good luck on your journey!

About the Co-Authors

Our name is Alex & George Kaplo; we're both certified personal trainers from Montreal, Canada. We will start by saying we are not the biggest guys you will ever meet, and this has never really been our goal. We started working out to overcome our biggest insecurity when we were younger, which was our self-confidence. You may be going through some challenges right now, or you may simply want to get fit, and we can certainly relate.

We always kind were interested in the health & fitness world and wanted to gain some muscle due to the numerous bullying in our teenage years. We figured we could do something about how our body looks like. This was the beginning of our transformation journey. We had no idea where to start, but we both just got started. We felt worried and afraid at times that other people would make fun of us for doing the exercises the wrong way. We always wished we had a friend to guide us and who could just show us the ropes.

After a lot of work, studying, and countless trials and errors. Some people began to notice how we were both getting more fit and how we were starting to form a keen interest in the topic. This led many friends and new faces to come to us and ask us for fitness advice. At first, it seemed odd when people asked us to help them get in shape. But what kept us going is when they started to see changes in their own body and told us it's the first time that they saw real results! From there, more people kept coming to us, and it made both of us realize after so much reading and studying in this field that it did help us, but it also allowed us to help others. To date, we have coached and trained numerous clients who have achieved some pretty amazing results.

Today, both of us own & operate this publishing business, where we bring passionate and expert authors to write about health and fitness topics. We also run an online fitness business, and we would love to connect with you by inviting you to visit the website on the following page and signing up for our e-mail newsletter (you will even get a free book).

Last but not least, if you are in the position we were once in and you want some guidance, don't hesitate and ask... I will be there to help you out!

Your coaches,

Alex & George Kaplo

Download another book for Free

We want to thank you for purchasing this book and offer you another book (just as long and valuable as this book), "Health & Fitness Mistakes You Don't Know You're Making," completely free.

Visit the link below to signup and receive it:

www.effingopublishing.com/gift

In this book, we will break down the most common health & fitness mistakes, you are probably committing right now, and will reveal how you can easily get in the best shape of your life!

In addition to this valuable gift, you will also have an opportunity to get our new books for free, enter giveaways, and receive other valuable emails from us. Again, visit the link to sign up:

www.effingopublishing.com/gift

Copyright 2019 by Effingo Publishing - All Rights Reserved.

This document by Effingo Publishing, owned by the A&G Direct Inc company, is geared towards providing exact and reliable information in regards to the topic and issue covered. The publication is sold with the idea that the publisher is not required to render accounting, officially permitted or otherwise qualified services. If advice is necessary, legal or professional, a practiced individual in the profession should be ordered.

From a Declaration of Principles which was accepted and approved equally by a Committee of the American Bar Association and a Committee of Publishers and Associations.

In no way is it legal to reproduce, duplicate, or transmit any part of this document in either electronic means or printed format. Recording of this publication is strictly prohibited, and any storage of this document is not allowed unless with written permission from the publisher. All rights reserved.

The information provided herein is stated to be truthful and consistent, in that any liability, in terms of inattention or otherwise, by any usage or abuse of any policies, processes, or directions contained within is the solitary and utter responsibility of the recipient reader. Under no circumstances will any legal responsibility or blame be held against the publisher for any reparation, damages, or monetary loss due to the information herein, either directly or indirectly.

The information herein is offered for informational purposes solely and is universal as so. The presentation of the information is without a contract or any type of guarantee assurance.

The trademarks that are used are without any consent, and the publication of the trademark is without permission or backing by the trademark owner. All trademarks and brands within this book are for clarifying purposes only and are owned by the owners themselves, not affiliated with this document.

For more great books, visit:

EffingoPublishing.com